D1398641

The Truth (& Myths) about Creepy Places

by L. A. Peacock

illustrated by Nick Wigsby

Benton Central Family Resource Center
905 Joe Creason Drive
Benton, KY 42025

Scholastic Inc.

To Naomi Schorr, my dear friend and a superb writer—L.A.F.

Photos ©: 5: North Wind Picture Archives; 12: Courtesy Salem Witch Museum; 13: Martin Gray/Getty Images; 15: Scott_Walton/Thinkstock; 21: Stephen Saks Photography/Alamy Images; 22: Larry MacDougal/iPhoto.ca/Newscom; 27: Pamela Bohnenstiehl; 28: AP Images; 29: AF archive/Alamy Images; 35: Robert Estall photo agency/Alamy Images; 41: Courtesy of the Collections of Louisiana State Museum; 42: Jack Young - Places/Alamy Images; 45: Jim West/Alamy Images; 47: Thomas Shjarback/Alamy Images; 49: Deejpilot/iStockphoto; 57: Nikreates/Alamy Images; 63: byllwill/iStockphoto; 68: Therealmaxim/Dreamstime; 71: Rob Goebel, The Indianapolis Star/AP Images; 73: Cincinnati Art Museum, Ohio, USA/Subscription Fund Purchase/Bridgeman Images; 77: Fortean/TopFoto/The Image Works; 78: Air Force/AP Images; 80: Fortean/TopFoto/The Image Works; 87: Joe Quinn/Alamy Images.

Text copyright © by L.A. Peacock
Illustrations copyright © 2015 by Scholastic Inc.
All rights reserved. Published by Scholastic Inc., *Publishers since 1920*.
SCHOLASTIC and associated logos are trademarks and/or registered trademarks of Scholastic Inc.

The publisher does not have any control over and does not assume any responsibility for author or third-party websites or their content.

No part of this publication may be reproduced, stored in a retrieval system, or transmitted in any form or by any means, electronic, mechanical, photocopying, recording, or otherwise, without written permission of the publisher. For information regarding permission, write to Scholastic Inc., Attention: Permissions Department, 557 Broadway, New York, NY 10012.

ISBN 978-0-545-83026-3

10 9 8 7 6 5 4 3 2 1   15 16 17 18 19/0

Printed in the U.S.A.   40

First edition, September 2015
Book design by David Neuhaus

Contents

Chapter 1
Witches of Salem, Massachusetts

What happened in this New England village in 1692?

Nineteen people went on **trial** for witchcraft. The trials began in Salem Village, about 30 miles north of Boston. The trouble quickly spread from Maine to New York.

How did the Salem witch trials begin?

Some young girls sat by the fire with the family's slave, Tituba. She told them African tales of talking animals and evil **demons**. Two of the girls, Betty and Abigail, later began to have strange fits, falling to the floor, screaming and kicking. Some adults said that the girls were under the **spell** of a witch. Soon, other girls started to act in the same way.

TITUBA SAID HER MOTHER WAS A WITCH.

SHE READ THE GIRLS' PALMS AND TOLD FORTUNES.

Did the girls get better?

No, they got worse. The girls began to have dreams. They saw spirits, or the shapes, of people. They **accused** Tituba and two other women, Sarah Good and Sarah Osborne, of being witches and causing them to act strangely.

Then what happened?

Arrests were made, and the accused people were brought to trial.

How many people were accused?

More than 150. Nineteen were hanged as witches, one was crushed to death with stones, and two died in prison.

Who was the youngest prisoner?

Dorcas Good, the five-year-old daughter of Sarah Good, an accused witch.

Why was Dorcas accused?

Little Dorcas had a red spot on her finger, which people believed was a mark from a snake who "talked to her." People said the snake was a witch's spirit companion, known as a "familiar."

What's a "familiar"?

Witches were believed to work spells from a distance. They could send a familiar spirit, a kind of devil in animal form, to do an evil job for them. Often familiars took the form of animals.

Were all the accused really witches?

No. The people who confessed were forgiven and released. Most of the others said they were innocent.

Could you prove you weren't a witch?

No. Even educated people believed in witches. Once suspected, it was your word against the people who accused you.

TRUTH or MYTH?

The Salem witches were burned at the stake.

MYTH! All nineteen convicted of witchcraft were hanged on Gallows Hill.

How could this witch hunt have happened?

Times were different in 17th-century colonial America. The Massachusetts colony was founded by pilgrims who left England with strong religious views. They believed that the devil was present on the earth and had strong power over people. Women believed to use magic to do the devil's work were known as witches.

WHEN BABIES DIED OR CROPS FAILED...

...EVIL SPIRITS WERE BLAMED!

Were there witch trials in England?

Yes. Witchcraft was a high crime in England, too.

What kind of evidence was presented in court?

Witnesses claimed that a serious injury was caused to them by "evil spirits" whom only they could see. People believed that a witch's spirit left her body and ran around the countryside causing trouble.

Why was it so easy to convict people as witches?

Judges at Salem accepted **spectral evidence** in the courtroom. Witnesses claimed to have seen the witch's "spectral shape," or spirit, in a dream. Sometimes, the accused person's body may have been miles away!

When were the witch trials over?

By the end of 1692, people began to question the use of spectral evidence. Governor William Phips allowed the trials to continue, but without using spectral evidence. Only three people were found guilty of twenty-one tried. A year later, the trials were over. Executions stopped and prisoners were set free.

TRUTH or MYTH?

An accused witch was last hanged in America in 1692.
TRUTH! But England's last witchcraft hanging was in 1713. Scotland's was in 1722.

What happened to Tituba?

Tituba was arrested on February 29, 1692, and taken to a Boston jail to await trial. She wasn't hanged because she had confessed that she was the devil's servant. It was what the judges wanted to hear!

Were Betty, Abigail, and the other afflicted girls under a witch's spell?

No, but they convinced themselves that witches were hurting them. Psychologists call this "group hysteria." This illness spreads from one person to another, like an idea that jumps from one mind to the next.

THE GIRLS ENJOYED THE ATTENTION THEY GOT...

IT WAS A GAME TO NAME THEIR NEIGHBORS AS WITCHES!

YOUR CREEPY PLACES I.Q.

The people in Salem kept evil spirits from their houses by . . .

a) surrounding their houses with sprigs of laurel

b) nailing a horseshoe over the front door

c) hanging a bone above each bed

d) wrapping something red around their necks

The answers are *a*, *b*, and *d*. They also hung a stone with a hole in the stable to protect livestock.

OUCH!

Why do many people visit Salem today?

Many come to tour the Salem Witch Museum. They learn about the famous witch trials. Life-sized figures show scenes of the accused people, trials, and hangings.

What other house in Salem can you visit?

The House of Seven Gables, the setting of Nathaniel Hawthorne's famous novel. The story is about Reverend Nicholas Noyes. He was cursed by the accused witch Sarah Good as she stood at the gallows.

HAWTHORNE WAS BORN IN SALEM IN 1804.

HE BELIEVED THE HOUSE WAS HAUNTED!

Chapter 2
Chaco Canyon, New Mexico

Where is the canyon located?

In northwestern New Mexico. It has the most pueblos in one place in the American Southwest. The site is the sacred ancestral homeland of today's Hopi and Pueblo peoples.

How big is the site?

Thirteen major buildings made of sandstone and **timber** remain.

What's special about the buildings?

Many of the structures were lined up to capture the cycles of the sun and moon. The ancient people of Chaco used their skills in **astronomy** to plan their city.

Who lived at Chaco Canyon long ago?

Native Americans called the Anasazi (ah-nah-SAH-zee).

How long did these Pueblo people live in the Southwest?

For more than two thousand years. They hunted with spears and gathered nuts, fruits, and berries. By 500 A.D., they had learned to plant crops and make pottery.

Who ruled the Anasazi?

Astronomers and priests were important leaders of this peaceful civilization.

How big was the Anasazi culture by the tenth century?

Huge! About 150 Anasazi villages joined together to form a great agricultural and religious center. The Anasazi built structures five stories tall with hundreds of rooms. Two hundred miles of wide roads connected the surrounding settlements.

The Anasazi used horses and wagons to move timber
to build their homes.

MYTH! They didn't have horses, mules, or wagons. The pine trees used for
building houses were up to 80 miles away. Tens of thousands of trees were
needed for the buildings.

How did they move so many pine logs?

Workers probably carried the heavy roof timbers along miles
of roads.

Did the Anasazi know a lot
of mathematics?

They must have. Their roads were built perfectly straight,
cutting through rocks and hills. Their buildings were designed
under overhanging cliffs. They were cool in the hot summer
and captured the sun's heat during winter. They built doorways
straight. Each stone was placed to follow a plan.

How did they use their knowledge of astronomy?

They created an astronomical **observatory** known as the Sun Dagger. The Anasazi also left behind many rock paintings and carvings of spiritual images. They built dozens of *kivas*, or round underground ceremonial chambers. These structures used solar energy and were perfectly lined up north-south.

How long did this amazing culture last?

About three hundred years. The Anasazi suddenly abandoned Chaco Canyon around 1250 A.D.

Why did they leave?

It's a mystery. The Anasazi left all their belongings, **sealed** the doors of their houses, and never returned. They migrated to other river valleys. Maybe they left because of lack of water, disease, or to escape an enemy tribe.

Are there any ghosts today at Chaco?

A strange naked one, according to some visitors and park employees. The ghost is surrounded by blue light. Some Hopi Indians believe that this giant spirit feeds off the energy of Mother Earth.

Where does this spirit live?

In the ground. He escapes from a sacred hole inside a ceremonial kiva. Some Indians believe these holes are connecting points to the Other Side, a world opposite to the one we are living in.

TRUTH or MYTH?

A park ranger once tried to arrest the naked spirit.
TRUTH! But he failed. He said the giant ghost disappeared into thin air!

HANDS UP!!!

What else creeps out visitors to Chaco?

Some tourists claim to hear bells and ancient people talking in the **ruins**.

What happens at night?

At sundown, fires are lit in the kivas. Some visitors say they feel shivers as spirits are released. Other people claim to see flashing lights and hear strange echoes in the ruins.

Are these feelings and sounds real?

Maybe. They might be caused by the earth's energy force known as **electromagnetism**.

Why is Chaco Canyon considered a sacred site?

It is the ancient home of today's Pueblo peoples. The ruins are also said to be located on one of the planet's centers of harmonic convergence. This is a place where changes in the earth's electromagnetic field sometimes occur. People who visit the site sometimes claim to have visions and see objects change color.

Chapter 3
Area 51, Nevada

What mystery lies along Highway 375 in the Nevada desert?

Area 51. It's a secret U.S. government military base between Highway 375 and Route 95 to the west.

How big is Area 51?

About 6 miles wide by 10 miles long. It borders the huge Nevada Test Site and Nellis Air Force Base.

Is Area 51 off-limits to ordinary people?

Yes, it's a **restricted zone**. Trespassers can be arrested, even shot to death, if they try to get in.

Why is Area 51 top secret?

Over many years, the government has developed **classified** national security projects here.

TRUTH or MYTH?

The U-2, a high-flying spy plane, was developed in Area 51.

TRUTH! The Pentagon admitted this in 1954. The plane was shot down by Soviet missiles on a spy mission over the Soviet Union in 1960.

What other spy aircraft came out of Area 51?

The SR-71 Blackbird spy plane, the B-2 bomber, and the F-117A stealth fighter.

How close can you get to Area 51?

In 1995, the government expanded the restricted zone, making it harder to see. To take a peek at the classified area, tourists go to Tikaboo Peak, about 25 miles away.

What can people see at night?

Eyewitnesses claim to see UFOs and other strange objects flying above Area 51. Some people say it's a secret flying-saucer base!

YOUR CREEPY PLACES I.Q.

What are other names for Area 51?

a) Freedom Ridge
b) Dreamland
c) Papoose Lake
d) The Alien Highway
e) White Sides

The answers are *a*, *b*, *c*, and *e*, all names of places in the restricted zone. The Alien Highway is the nickname for Highway 375

How do we know about Area 51 projects?

In 1989, government scientist Bob Lazar spoke on a TV show. He claimed Area 51 was a secret flying-saucer base. He said his job was to study alien crafts to see how they worked. The government's plan was to use the aliens' advanced technology in future U.S. planes.

Did Lazar see any flying saucers?

He said he saw nine. The UFOs had crashed or been captured. Lazar claimed to have witnessed the test flight of one these saucers flown by an Air Force pilot.

Was Lazar telling the truth?

We don't know. Lazar was fired for talking about the secret projects.

What happened after Lazar's TV interview?

UFO believers rushed to the borders of Area 51. They made Little A'Le'Inn (or "Little Alien"), a small restaurant and motel in nearby Rachel, Nevada, their headquarters. Tourists can buy UFO tapes, books, T-shirts, and other souvenirs there.

Do people live in Rachel, Nevada?

About fifty people. The **residents** have to put up with loud sonic booms from Area 51's jet aircraft. The noises have caused pictures to fall off walls and knickknacks to fly off shelves.

Can people visit Area 51?

No, but tourists can sign up for a hiking trip to Tikaboo Peak. Tours near Area 51 are advertised in UFO magazines.

Have people actually seen flying saucers?

Hundreds of witnesses have claimed to see bright lights in the area. The lights hover for a while, then streak across the night sky and vanish. Other visitors report seeing bright objects that jump around in the sky.

What do experts say about Area 51?

One UFO researcher, Sean Morton, says he views UFOs regularly. On a good night, he can see "anywhere between twenty to forty objects." But most scientists explain the sightings as shooting stars, satellites, or tests by the military of new aircraft.

Who was Mercy Brown?

A nineteen-year-old farmer's daughter who died in January 1892. Some people believed that her death was caused by a vampire's kiss. Today, Mercy Brown is known by some as the last North American vampire.

Where is she buried?

In the family plot in Chestnut Hill Cemetery in Exeter, Rhode, Island.

What are vampires?

In folk tradition, vampires are **corpses**, or dead bodies, that come to life. They are evil beings who feed on the blood of living creatures. Vampires sometimes visit loved ones and cause trouble.

How do we know about vampires today?

Mostly from books and magazines, such as Bram Stoker's 1897 novel *Dracula*.

Are all vampires creepy looking?

Not all of them. Just ask Bella from the popular *Twilight* books and movies.

Which writer from New Orleans helped make vampires famous?

Anne Rice, best known for her Vampire Chronicles books. She grew up in New Orleans, Louisiana, and moved back there in the late 1980s. Her old **mansion** was for sale for $2.65 million. But buyers beware—the old house is said to be haunted!

What did Mercy Brown really die of?

She suffered from tuberculosis, or TB.

What do people with TB look like?

Victims of the disease often turn pale, stop eating, and lose lots of weight. Blood collects in their lungs. They can wake up at night with blood on their faces and necks from coughing. People easily made a connection between vampires of legend and TB victims.

IN THE 1800s, ONE OUT OF FOUR PEOPLE DIED FROM TB.

IT WAS CALLED CONSUMPTION THEN.

What did her family suspect after Mercy died?

Her father believed that Mercy was responsible for the death of his wife and oldest daughter. He was convinced that the vampire Mercy Brown was now attacking Edwin, her brother, who was also dying of tuberculosis.

Why did her father dig up Mercy's grave?

He wanted proof that she was a vampire. He planned to drive a stake through Mercy's heart, remove her internal organs, and burn her body to ashes. This **ritual**, as folklore once said, would rid the town of evil and cure Edwin.

What did he find?

There wasn't much **decomposition**. Mercy looked pretty good, even though her body was not **embalmed**.

Did the doctor remove her organs?

Yes, and he found blood in her liver and heart. This was proof to her father that Mercy was a vampire.

TRUTH or MYTH?

Evidence was also found that Mercy had moved in her coffin.

TRUTH! Mercy was not embalmed. When bodies decompose, they sometimes seem to move, because gases are released naturally in decomposition.

Why did her father burn Mercy's heart and liver?

To keep her from rising from the dead.

SOME BELIEVE THAT YOU KILL A VAMPIRE BY DESTROYING ITS HEART!

THE EVIL SPELL IS BROKEN!

What did Mercy's father do with the ashes?

He made medicine from Mercy's ashes for the dying Edwin. According to folklore, the victim would get well.

Did the medicine work?

No, the **remedy** failed. Edwin died two months later.

Why did Mercy's neighbors believe the cure worked?

There were no more vampires in Exeter. Mercy Brown was the last reported in recent times.

Is the grave of Mercy Brown haunted?

Some people think so. Visitors claim to see Mercy's ghost near her headstone.

What else do witnesses say?

Some report seeing a strange blue light moving through the cemetery. They believe it's Mercy's spirit, now free from her grave.

Chapter 5
Mystery Hill, New Hampshire

What sits on top of a remote hill in Salem, New Hampshire?

A mysterious site built of heavy stones. Some people think it's one of the first—and oldest—man-made **constructions** in America.

How big is the site?

About one hundred acres. There are low, winding stone walls and crude cavelike buildings. Some of the stones weigh up to eleven tons. People believe that they were placed with care and purpose by ancient people who knew about stonework and astronomy.

Why is it called America's Stonehenge?

England's Stonehenge consists of a ring of giant stones on a flat, open plain. It was built thousands of years ago by ancient people. Even today, both sites remain mysteries.

STONEHENGE, ENGLAND

How does Stonehenge compare with Mystery Hill?

Both structures were built to observe solar and lunar events. However, Stonehenge and Mystery Hill were built very differently.

TRUTH or MYTH?

Mystery Hill was built by ancient Vikings.

MYTH! The Vikings may have first visited North America in the late 900s A.D. But Mystery Hill is much older than that, and there is no evidence that the Vikings built it or lived there.

How old is Mystery Hill?

Pottery at the site dated back to about 1000 B.C. Charcoal from the fire pit tested to be about four thousand years old.

Did astronomers work there?

Probably. The stone buildings line up to show yearly events of the sun and moon. Nearby stones mark the change of seasons and the directions of the compass.

Could aliens have built Mystery Hill?

Some UFO believers claim that the stonework could be a giant map, a "landing **beacon**" for visiting aliens. They think the markings on some stones could be messages from visitors from outer space.

What other ancient peoples could have built the site?

Some people believe that the ancient Phoenicians created Mystery Hill and the writing on the stones. The Phoenicians lived about 1200 B.C. to 146 B.C. They sailed and traded over great distances.

Why is the site still a mystery?

Some people don't believe the **theory** about the Phoenicians. They ask why these faraway sailors would travel twenty-five miles inland to settle on a hill. And there is no real proof that the carved lines on the stones are Phoenician writing.

What's the creepiest part of Mystery Hill?

At the center of the site is a large flat stone. It looks like a table on four stone legs. People attending a ceremony there might have believed they could hear voices of dead spirits. Behind the table, there's a hidden eight-foot-long tube leading to an underground room. A priest could sit there and speak through the tube in an **eerie** voice and give predictions or commands.

Who discovered Mystery Hill?

Early American colonists came upon the strange stone ruins and named it Mystery Hill. In 1826, a farmer, Jonathan Pattee, built a house over the stoneworks. He sold some of the flat rocks to local builders.

STONES FOR SALE

Can you visit the site today?

Yes, the Stone family of Derry, New Hampshire, bought the place. They opened America's Stonehenge Park to the public in 1958.

Who was known as the Voodoo Queen of New Orleans?

Marie Laveau. She was a descendant of African slaves but was herself a free woman. In the 1830s, Marie practiced voodoo, a religion that uses spells and magic.

What kind of magic did she practice?

Marie sold love **potions** and charms to cure illnesses from her home. She often led voodoo dances in New Orleans's Congo Square.

TRUTH or MYTH?

Marie Laveau discovered a Fountain of Youth, because she never seemed to grow old.

MYTH! There were *two* Laveaus. People often confused Marie with her daughter, who looked just like her. The mother died in 1880; her daughter ten years later.

Where are they buried?

The two tombs are in Saint Louis Cemetery, an old graveyard in New Orleans's French Quarter.

What was creepy about Marie's appearance?

She hardly seemed to age. In her eighties, Marie was still holding voodoo ceremonies. She looked as young as she did when she started.

Why do people visit the Laveau graves?

Some of them believe in voodoo and seek Marie's help. Visitors often mark the two graves with three Xs for good luck. They leave messages and offerings of coins and flowers.

What happens when you knock on the graves three times?

Some people believe that you might call up the ghost of Marie Laveau!

Did Marie have special powers over the weather?

The police thought so at the time. Marie is said to have saved several criminals from hanging. She created a spell so a violent storm appeared. The heavy rains made the ropes slip off the convicted men's necks, so they fell safely through the gallows's trapdoor.

Where do people most often see Marie's ghost?

Along St. Ann Street, near her house. The spirit is said to wear a long white dress and a handkerchief of seven knots around her neck.

Did Marie's daughter live in the French Quarter, too?

Yes. Her house today is now a voodoo shop.

Are there other ghosts in the French Quarter?

Some think so. A famous haunted house belonged to General Beauregard (BO-ruh-gard). He fought for the South in the Civil War.

What sometimes happens at his house around 2 A.M.?

Witnesses claim to see the ghosts of Beauregard and his troops. They are reliving the Battle of Shiloh.

What do the ghosts look like?

The soldiers are said to wear their old uniforms. Their clothes are torn and bloody. Some visitors claim to hear the sounds of battle echoing in the hallways.

What famous pirate lived in New Orleans?

Jean Lafitte. He led his pirates to rob and attack British and Spanish ships along the Gulf Coast, from Texas to Louisiana, in the early 1800s.

Where did he hide the gold he stole?

Some people believe Lafitte buried his pirate treasure under the fireplace in the family blacksmith shop. Today, the shop is a famous bar in the French Quarter.

What creepy things happen at the bar?

Some visitors claim to see the old pirate roaming the halls. The lights mysteriously turn on and off. Other witnesses report seeing glowing red eyes in the fireplace.

Who lives at 1600 Pennsylvania Avenue?

That's the address of the White House, home of the president of the United States and the first family.

Who else lives there?

Some people believe the White House is haunted by famous ghosts. Many are former presidents and their wives.

Where are the ghosts hiding?

Everywhere, according to believers. The ghost of President William Henry Harrison can be heard stomping around the attic. Some White House workers have witnessed the ghost of President John Adams's wife, Abigail, hanging her laundry in the East Room. Some say they can smell the damp clothes and soap.

When was the White House built?

Construction started in 1792. The original building had sixty-four rooms on three levels.

Who built the White House?

Mostly slaves from local **plantations** and skilled immigrants. The stone walls were built four feet thick, with fancy windows and whitewashed walls outside.

TRUTH or MYTH?

George Washington was the first president to live in the White House.

MYTH! Washington supervised the design and building of "The People's House" but he never lived in it.

JOHN ADAMS WAS THE FIRST PRESIDENT TO LIVE IN THE WHITE HOUSE.

JOHN AND ABIGAIL SPENT THE FIRST NIGHT THERE ON NOVEMBER 1, 1800.

Who planted the White House Rose Garden?

Dolley Madison, the wife of James Madison, the fourth president.

When did Dolley's ghost first appear?

Some say during the administration of Woodrow Wilson, the twenty-eighth president. One hundred years after Dolley planted the garden, Mrs. Wilson gave orders to have the garden dug up. But some people believe that Dolley's ghost appeared and, as witnesses said, stopped the workers. The Rose Garden is still there, just outside the Oval Office. Presidential press conferences are often held there today.

HAVE YOU SEEN THE GHOST OF DOLLEY MADISON?

TRUTH or MYTH?

The White House was set on fire by a ghost during the War of 1812.

MYTH! There were reports of the ghost of a soldier carrying a torch. But the British army actually set the fire when they invaded Washington, D.C.

AFTER THE FIRE, ONLY FOUR WALLS REMAINED.

EVERYTHING INSIDE THE WHITE HOUSE WAS BURNT TO ASHES.

DOLLEY MADISON WAS ABLE TO SAVE A FAMOUS PAINTING OF GEORGE WASHINGTON.

What other presidents haunt the White House?

Witnesses say the ghost of Andrew Jackson occupies the Rose Bedroom. An **aide** to President Lyndon Johnson heard Jackson's ghost hollering there in 1964. Others believe that Thomas Jefferson's ghost still haunts the White House. Visitors claim to hear him play his violin in empty rooms.

Who was the first to see the ghost of Abraham Lincoln?

Grace, the wife of Calvin Coolidge, the 30th president. She claimed to see Lincoln in a window in the Yellow Oval Room on the second floor. Lincoln's ghost was standing, with his hands clasped behind him. When alive, President Lincoln spent a lot of time thinking while gazing out this window.

YOUR CREEPY PLACES I.Q.

Who else reported feeling the presence of Lincoln's ghost?

a) President Harry Truman

b) First Lady Eleanor Roosevelt

c) Winston Churchill

d) President Johnson's daughter Lynda Johnson Robb

The answers are *a*, *b*, and *c*. Lynda reported feeling the spirit of Willie Lincoln, the president's young son who died in the White House from typhoid fever in 1862.

Who tried to talk to
Willie Lincoln's ghost?

His mother. Mary Todd Lincoln regularly held meetings with fortune-tellers in the White House. She tried to contact the spirit of her dead son to help her overcome her grief.

Did President Lincoln also believe
in the supernatural?

Maybe. He often attended his wife's meetings with **psychics**. Witnesses said that, at one session, the president ordered a congressman to sit on a piano that was floating above the floor!

Could Lincoln predict the future?

Lincoln is reported to have had a vision of his own **assassination** ten days before he was shot on April 14, 1865.

TRUTH or MYTH?

Queen Wilhelmina of the Netherlands claimed to have seen Lincoln's ghost in 1945.

TRUTH! She was sleeping across the hall from the Lincoln Bedroom when she heard a knock. She opened her door. There according to the queen stood the ghost of Abraham Lincoln in his top hat!

Does Lincoln's ghost still haunt the White House?

Some overnight guests in the Lincoln Bedroom have a hard time sleeping. They claim to have seen the president's ghost hovering over the nine-foot-long bed.

Chapter 8
Pirates' House, Georgia

When was the house built?

In 1754, by sailors. It was originally a tavern. Seamen came to Savannah, Georgia, from **ports** all over the world.

How was it made?

The original structure was made of wooden beams, held together by wooden pegs, just the way sailors build ships. Today, it's a famous local restaurant.

TRUTH or MYTH?

The famous pirate Bluebeard once lived here.

MYTH! Bluebeard didn't, but Jean Lafitte did. But Lafitte and his wife came at a later time.

Who is said to haunt Pirates' House today?

The ghost of another famous pirate known as Captain Flint.

What does Captain Flint's ghost cry out for?

Witnesses say the pirate's spirit keeps calling out for his first mate, Darby McGraw, to bring him some rum. To this day, some visitors to the restaurant hear his ghostly cries.

How do we know about Captain Flint?

Mostly from the novel *Treasure Island*. Robert Lewis Stevenson wrote about the **notorious** pirate Captain Flint in his famous book. He even called Bluebeard "a child" compared to the bloodthirsty Captain Flint.

WHAT WERE FLINT'S LAST WORDS?

"FETCH AFT THE RUM, DARBY!"

Where is Captain Flint's ghost most often seen?

In the basement of Pirates' House. Not surprising, because that's where kegs of rum were stored.

What was discovered in the rum cellar?

A wide tunnel leading from Pirates' House to the nearby Savannah River.

Why was the tunnel kept a secret?

It was a getaway for pirates to escape to the sea.

Who else used the tunnel?

Press gangs. These were groups of men whose job was to kidnap sailors and force them to work on sailing ships. If press gangs couldn't find anybody on the streets, they went to Pirates' House. It was easy to capture drunken men and then drag them through the tunnel out to sea.

Are there ghosts at Pirates' House today?

Some people think so. Pirates' House is now a restaurant. Visitors have reported seeing the ghost of a burly ship captain eating at a table. Mysteriously, the captain would get up and vanish!

What are other signs of pirate hauntings?

Restaurant workers say they hear mysterious noises, such as footsteps, banging on walls, and exploding glassware.

Can tourists visit Pirates' House?

Visitors to Savannah can book a dinner reservation or take the "Creepy Crawl Haunted Pub Tour," which starts at Pirates' House.

How did Death Valley get its name?

From the **survivors** of a group of thirty pioneers trying to cross the Mojave Desert in 1849. Twelve of them died from the extreme heat. Even today, Death Valley looks like the dry and rocky surface of the moon.

How hot does it get?

Temperatures can reach 134 degrees Fahrenheit.

THAT'S AN AMERICAN RECORD SET ON JULY 10, 1913.

DEATH VALLEY GOT ITS NAME DURING THE CALIFORNIA GOLD RUSH OF 1849.

What mystery lies under the surface of Death Valley?

A lot of hidden deep **caverns** and tunnels—at least thirty-two of them, covering about 180 square miles of Death Valley and parts of southern Nevada.

Who discovered the underground cavern near Wingate Pass?

Dr. F. Bruce Russell, a retired Ohio doctor, in 1931. He was looking for gold when he broke through the surface and fell headfirst into a cave.

What did Russell claim to find in the cave?

The skeletons of gigantic men, each about eight feet tall. Russell reported that these mummylike bodies were dressed in jackets and pants made out of animal skins.

How was Russell able to see the bodies in such a dark place?

He said the caves were illuminated by a mysterious green light.

THE LIGHT PROBABLY CAME FROM UNDERGROUND NATURAL GAS.

What else did Russell find in the caves?

He claimed to see the bones of tigers and elephants scattered across the floor of the cavern. These were likely the remains of ancient saber-tooth tigers and mammoths.

TRUTH or MYTH?

Scientists believed Dr. Russell had discovered an ancient civilization of giant men.

MYTH! They laughed at his stories. They needed to see evidence.

What happened to Dr. Russell?

He returned to Death Valley to get proof of his discovery. But Dr. Russell vanished in the ancient caves, never to be seen again.

Who else explored these deep caves?

Bourke Lee, a Death Valley historian, told a similar story that he heard from two men in 1932. The men said they had also fallen by accident through the thin surface soil into a huge cavern.

Did these men find giant skeletons, too?

No, but they said they found several mummified men of regular size. These mummies were sitting upright, holding gold spears in their hands. Around them were walls, doors, and tables—all made of gold!

What happened to this secret city of gold?

No one knows. The men told Lee that they were going back to the ancient city. But Lee never heard from them again. Like Dr. Russell, the men vanished in the mysterious tunnels and caves of Death Valley.

What other mystery brings tourists to Death Valley?

Visitors often come to Racetrack Playa, a flat area next to an 850-foot-high hillside of **dolomites**. They are amazed to see large stones and rocks that seem to have moved across the flat desert floor, as if by magic.

How far have the stones appeared to have traveled?

Hundreds of feet across the desert floor. They left behind grooves, tracks, and marks of rocks as they flipped over.

THE ROCKS WEIGH UP TO 650 POUNDS.

SOME LEFT TRAILS UP TO 1,500 FEET LONG.

YOUR CREEPY PLACES I.Q.

Scientists believe the rocks moved by natural forces, such as

a) magnetic and gravity forces

b) a water slick on the dry clay surface

c) supernatural forces

d) the power of wind

The answers are *a*, *b*, and *d*. Most **geologists** agree that weather or earth forces caused the curious movement of the rocks, not magic.

TRUTH or MYTH?

People report seeing ghosts of camels in Death Valley.

TRUTH! In 1855, the U.S. Army bought camels from Turkey to replace pack horses. Camels could better survive the high temperatures of the desert and lack of regular water. Some people today report seeing their ghosts.

What happened to the camels?

Most were eaten by Civil War soldiers, who were starved for meat. Some camels went to zoos and circuses. Others were released into the desert. The last wild camel was seen in the U.S. Southwest in 1941.

What about the camels' ghosts?

In the 1950s, Fat Mack Mahoney, a **prospector** in Death Valley, said he came across a herd of seven camels on a hot afternoon. As he moved closer, he watched them vanish into "a hazy green fog."

Who else saw a camel ghost?

In 1962, Wendell Bishop was at Racetrack Playa when he saw a camel fifty feet away. On top was a rider dressed in a Civil War army uniform. Suddenly, the vision of the camel and its rider disappeared!

Chapter 10
Hannah House, Indiana

When was the grand house built?

In 1858. The twenty-four-room red brick mansion was built by Alexander Hannah.

HANNAH WAS A POSTMASTER AND SHERIFF.

HE SERVED AS CLERK OF THE CIRCUIT COURT.

Why do people say Hannah House is haunted?

Because many strange things happen here. Ghosts are said to roam the halls. Visitors experience smells of rotting **flesh**, mysterious cold spots, and crashing glassware.

TRUTH or MYTH?

Hannah House was part of the Underground Railroad.
TRUTH! Before the Civil War, Hannah used his home as a secret "safe house" for runaway slaves.

What was the Underground Railroad?

It was a series of secret routes and safe houses used by 19th-century slaves on their way to free states and Canada. Escaped slaves moved north in secret, from one safe house to the next.

Who ran the safe houses and helped runaway slaves?

Abolitionists. These were men and women who believed all people were equal. They risked their lives to help bring an end to slavery in America.

AT NIGHT, HANNAH LOADED SLAVES INTO WAGONS ...

... AND BROUGHT THEM TO THE NEXT SAFE HOUSE.

How many slaves escaped this way?

By 1850, about 100,000 had taken the Underground Railroad to freedom.

Where did Hannah hide the slaves?

In the basement of his house. Some people claim to see the ghosts of these slaves still hiding there.

Did any slaves die in Hannah House?

Some did, tragically. A lantern in the basement was knocked over, setting the house on fire. The flames killed several slaves. Later, the house was rebuilt. Some people believe that the ghosts of the dead slaves haunt the house today.

What is the creepiest thing about the house?

The sickening smell of rotten flesh coming from a second-floor bedroom. Psychics say that the smell comes from the spirit of Hannah's dead unborn child. The ghost of Hannah himself was supposedly seen in 1972, standing near the second-floor stairway.

Have people lived in Hannah House in recent times?

Yes, John and Gladys O'Brien sold antiques and lived there from 1968 to 1978.

Did John and Gladys see ghosts?

They often were bothered by Hannah hauntings. They heard mysterious noises and smelled strange odors. Their youngest daughter claimed to have seen the ghost of an old man walk up the stairs and then vanish!

What did a local TV crew witness?

Strange activities. They were at Hannah House one Halloween. The TV crew was there to film a psychic walking through the spooky house. She claimed to feel mysterious cold spots, indicating that ghosts were nearby.

What else did the cameraman witness?

Something mysterious. He looked up and pointed at an old **chandelier** on the ceiling. Just then it moved, swinging back and forth on its own. There was no breeze in the room, and all the doors and windows were shut.

IT'S MOVING!!!

Have these strange happenings been explained?

Not yet, but ghost hunters continue to investigate the old mansion.

NO HIDDEN WIRES WERE ATTACHED TO THE CHANDELELIER.

THERE WERE SEVEN WITNESSES TO THIS SPOOKY EVENT.

Chapter 11
Roswell, New Mexico

What strange event took place the night of July 2, 1947?

Local rancher William Brazel heard a huge explosion near the army airfield. The next morning, he found pieces of metal on his property.

What was mysterious about the metal?

It was super strong but weighed little. Brazel couldn't dent the pieces, even with a sledgehammer.

Did a UFO crash at Roswell?

Some people thought so. The army came to collect the **debris**. Everything was kept locked up in Hangar 84 at the base.

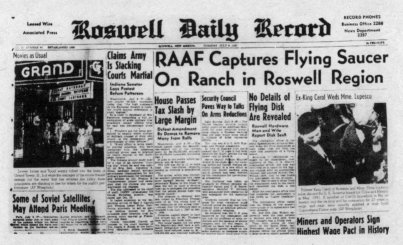

What else did the army find at the site?

Some people claimed that four strange-looking bodies were also taken away for examination.

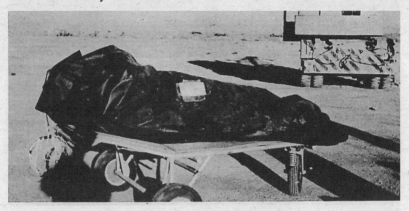

TRUTH or MYTH?

The army said they had evidence of "flying discs."
TRUTH! It was in the first report. But later, the army denied the debris came from an alien aircraft.

BUT RUMORS SPREAD...

MAYBE THE GOVERNMENT FOUND A SPACESHIP WITH ALIEN BODIES!

How did the army explain the debris?

The military claimed it came from a top-secret balloon device, code-named Mogul. The craft was designed to spy on Soviet nuclear tests.

Was the government hiding the truth?

Some UFO experts thought so. They believed the military had actually found an entire spaceship with aliens onboard.

What did the military say about the bodies found at the site?

They explained that they were crash-test dummies, the same kind they used when testing high-altitude aircraft.

PEOPLE SAY IT WAS A GOVERNMENT COVER-UP!

VISITORS COME TO ROSWELL TO LEARN THE TRUTH ABOUT THE ALIEN CRASH.

Was the government holding back information?

We may never know. All the official files on the Roswell crash were **shredded** by unknown persons.

What happened to the place where the alien bodies were said to be examined in 1947?

A new brick building replaced the old wooden structure. It was renamed the New Mexico Rehabilitation Center (NMRC).

Is the new NMRC haunted?

Some people claim that the alien spirits of the UFO crash live here.

Why is the NMRC staff afraid to go on the second floor?

This is where UFO researchers claim the alien bodies were studied in 1947. The old building was gone, but some people believed that ghosts remained on the second floor.

What unexplained incidents did the NMRC staff report?

a) elevators mysteriously opening and closing

b) strange footsteps along the corridors

c) lights flashing on and off

d) alien ghosts in empty beds

The answers are *a*, *b*, and *c*. They didn't see spirits in beds, but some did report seeing the ghost of a World War II pilot roaming the corridors.

Can tourists visit Hangar 84 at the Roswell airfield?

Yes. It's the place where the alien bodies were said to be first kept. Some visitors go there to try to communicate with the dead aliens.

Did a camera crew film at Hangar 84?

Yes, a Discovery Channel film crew was there in November 2005. They were filming for an unsolved mystery TV show.

Who visited with them?

A group of psychics. They formed a circle around a table. Their eyes were closed and they held hands. They were trying to contact the alien spirits.

What did the camera team say they saw when they viewed the film?

A horrible, snakelike creature twisting above the heads of the psychics. Moments later, as the film showed, the creature disappeared!

Did the Discovery Channel show the program?

No, it never made it on air. To this day, some of the crew believe they had captured a supernatural event on film.

Where is one of the most haunted places in the U.S.?

In South Carolina's Georgetown County. Spirits are said to wander the graveyards, manor houses, and estates along the coast and nearby Pawleys Island.

Why are ghosts said to be attracted to Georgetown County?

Many powerful events happened here. Families and plantations were destroyed in the Revolutionary War and the Civil War. People lost their lives to diseases and hurricanes. Brave soldiers and young lovers met tragic deaths. Some believe that only their ghosts remain to tell their stories.

Do ghosts like visitors?

Some town officials believe so. They offer popular tours of haunted plantations, cemeteries, and mansions.

Who are the ghosts?

Alice Flagg is one of the most famous. Sixteen-year-old Alice lived with her older brother Allard. A wealthy doctor, Allard built the Hermitage, the family mansion, in 1848.

What was Alice's secret?

She fell in love with and got engaged to a traveling salesman. She wore her engagement ring around her neck to hide it from her brother.

Did her brother find the ring?

Suffering from malaria, Alice lay on her deathbed. Allard saw the ring on her necklace. In anger, he tore it off and threw the ring away.

TRUTH or MYTH?

Alice got her ring back.

MYTH! Alice begged for the ring before she died, but it was never returned to her.

Where have some reported seeing Alice's ghost?

At nearby All Saints Cemetery in the Flagg family plot. Her gravestone is marked with only one word: Alice.

What is her ghost said to look like?

A pretty teenager. She appears in a long white dress, the same one she was buried in.

Who made the dirt path circling Alice's grave?

The many visitors who walk backward around her grave thirteen times. They hope to awaken Alice's spirit by following this ritual.

Why is her grave covered with flowers and small notes?

Many are left by romantic teenagers. Some people believe that a few flowers are placed there by the ghost of her dead brother.

Where else have tourists reported seeing Alice's ghost?

Looking out the round window of her second-floor bedroom. Some say her spirit has returned from the dead to look for her lost ring.

Who haunts Huntington Beach State Park?

The ghost of a ten-year-old boy. Visitors to the beach claim to hear him cry out for help.

When did the boy die?

In the 1930s. A huge stone crab is said to have grabbed his arms and held him down. The boy drowned when the **tide** came in. Nobody heard his cries above the noise of the surf pounding the shore.

What ghost haunts the manor house of Wedgefield Plantation?

Some believe it is the spirit of a headless British soldier who died in 1781. He was guarding the house during the American Revolutionary War.

Who killed him?

Francis Marion, the legendary Swamp Fox. This American rebel leader used his sharp sword to cut off the British soldier's head. Witnesses say his headless body staggered about, then fell, like a chicken that had just lost its head.

Where was the soldier buried?

In the garden. His headless ghost was said to be seen roaming the grounds, pistol in hand, searching for his head!

NOW, WHERE DID I LEAVE IT??

Which three ghosts walk the roads of Pawleys Island?

Witnesses have claimed to see the spirits of a Civil War soldier, a bride, and a groom.

What happened at nearby Hagley Plantation?

The soldier, believed to be dead, surprised his sweetheart on the night of her wedding to another man. The soldier was so sad about her marriage that he drowned himself in the ocean. When the bride found out, she jumped off a dock to her own death. Out of grief, the groom committed suicide, too.

IT WAS A TRIPLE SUICIDE.

THEIR GHOSTS STILL HAUNT HAGLEY PLANTATION.

What ghost appears just before dangerous storms?

The Gray Man, as locals call him. He wears a gray cap and clothes.

TRUTH or MYTH?

The Gray Man is said to be the ghost of a young man who died in 1800.

TRUTH! He was riding to see his fiancée on Pawleys Island. But his horse tripped and threw him into a pit of quicksand. He drowned.

What happened to his fiancée?

She was heartbroken. One day, she saw a man dressed in gray, walking on the beach. Suddenly, he disappeared.

Did her family believe she saw a ghost?

No, they took her to a doctor sixty miles away. Hours later, a hurricane hit the island and destroyed most of the houses. Today, people claim that the Gray Man's appearance is a warning of a bad storm coming.

Match the Georgetown ghosts to their haunting places:

1) Gray Man   a) Huntington Beach
2) Alice Flagg   b) Hagley Plantation
3) Civil War soldier   c) Pawleys Island
4) Crab Boy   d) Wedgefield Manor
5) Headless soldier   e) Hermitage

The answers are 1c, 2e, 3b, 4a, and 5d. Pawleys Island is also the home of the triple-suicide ghosts.

Glossary

abolitionist—a person in favor of ending a law or system, such as slavery

accuse—to say that a person has done something wrong or is guilty of something

aide—a person who helps another person in his or her job

assassination—the murder of a famous person for political reasons

astronomy—the scientific study of the sun, moon, stars, and planets

beacon—a light that guides vehicles or warns them of danger

cavern—a large cave

chandelier—a fancy round light with branches for holding small bulbs or candles that hangs from the ceiling

classified—officially secret and open only to particular people

construction—the way something has been built or made

corpse—a dead body

debris—pieces of brick, wood, and metal that are left after something has been destroyed

decomposition—state of being destroyed gradually by natural chemical processes

demon—an evil spirit

dolomite—a kind of large rock made mostly of a calcium material

eerie—strange, mysterious, and frightening

electromagnetism—the production of a magnetic field by means of an electric current

embalm—to prevent a dead body from decaying by treating it with special chemicals to preserve it

evidence—support or proof that something is true

flesh—the skin of the human body

geologist—a scientist who studies the earth, rocks, and soil

mansion—a large, fancy house

notorious—well known for being bad

observatory—a special building to watch the stars

plantation—a large area of land where crops such as coffee and cotton are grown

port—a city with a harbor where ships load and unload goods

potion—a drink or liquid with magic powers

prospector—a person who searches an area for gold or other minerals

psychic—a person who claims to have the power to predict the future or to speak to dead people

remedy—a treatment or medicine to cure a disease

resident—a person who lives in a particular place

restricted zone—an area controlled by special rules or laws

ritual—something that is always done in the same way

ruins—the parts of a building that remain after it has been badly damaged or destroyed

seal—to close tightly to keep out air or water

shredded—something that is cut or torn into small pieces

spectral—like a ghost or spirit

spell—words that are believed to have magic power

survivor—a person who continues to live despite being nearly killed

theory—an opinion or idea that somebody believes but that is not proven

tide—the regular rise and fall in the level of the sea

timber—trees that are grown for building things

trial—examining evidence before a judge and often a jury, to decide if somebody is guilty of a crime